SNOW ON A CROCUS

Formalities of a Neonaticide

For Noel
with love
Joan
august 9, 2010

Joan Swift

The Walter Pavlich Memorial Poetry Award 2010

ISBN 978-1-930454-27-9

Swan Scythe Press
515 P Street #804
Sacramento CA 95814
http://www.swanscythepress.com

Editors: James DenBoer and Sandra McPherson
Book Design: Mark Deamer
Cover Art: Imao Keinen
Cover Design: Mark Deamer

For C.S.

Contents

So now the Slumberer inside me has,
Secretly, returned....

from "Song," by Tomas Tranströmer,
translated by Robert Hass,
Time and Materials

What Comes Back

There is no face, no hair, no skin smell,
searing blue or liquid brown eyes telling me
here's the one I killed.
I float in gauze as day begins its shape
around the bed. There is no blood,
no thud of a falling body,
yet I wake up sure I've killed someone.
My victim waits outside the shower
while water tries to rinse the ghost away.
Did I kill my father? He vanished when I was six.

Or was it the man who raped me years ago?
He got off with an easy plea, five years in Vacaville,
then he raped again and killed. Her name was Joan.
Her jacket was the color of a lime and his semen ran
a silver river over it. When I took the stand
I told the jury how I painted a windowsill that day
he lunged in through the door, how he grabbed my throat
and threw me down. The jury gave him life.
Is he the one I killed?

March, gray Sunday morning. My cousin phones:
her granddaughter…baby girl born in a dorm room…
wrapping of the child in plastic…dumpster
behind that empty place of love and tears and terror.
I sink into the texture of the chair. I mourn.
Is there a killer waiting in all of us?

II

I pull my coat around me...I rock and
lament my foolish ways, but even if I had been wise I would have failed
to change my fate;

Lament my foolishness then and later and now, for which I would like
so much to be forgiven.

Czeslaw Milosz
New and Collected Poems 1931-2001

Hundreds of neonaticides occur each year...
Societal institutions and the professionals who
run them have failed to acknowledge the patterned
nature of this phenomenon, and have sought
instead to haphazardly blame such crimes solely
on the individuals who commit them.

Cheryl L. Meyer and Michelle Oberman
Mothers Who Kill Their Children

The Start of the Story and Some of the End

You walk through waterfalls all afternoon
and rainbows made of the drenched sun.

There is enchantment
where you step through yarrow, aster, mint.

A spell falls over you and love
is nothing else but lying down, a dove

on each of your bare toes and on his back
a tee shirt you keep pulling on like

a bell for all the ringing. Later
snow will fall on your mother's hair

as she walks from her car to the courtroom.
Killing is always the same.

The child will circle your days long after she's gone
like a boat that swings on an anchor chain

and never heads out to sea
day after trembling day.

Journey

You know his baby is inside you when you smell the
    French fries
he passes from the frozen custard stand right under your
    nose.

He has the lake's grace — the rough and shove of a wind-
    blown wave
and the transparent running of water up the shore's
    concave

bowl of sand. Your stomach lurches but you don't let him
    know
when he hands you a hot dog through the car window,

your black running back making this touchdown.
Woman in love on a late summer afternoon,

you pull your fingers through the light strands of your hair
and try not to tell him a baby is there

suddenly between you. Exiled Pacific salmon are just
    begin-
ing their run from the lake, scales that could be sun

on the small creek's surface or leaves blowing over, cop-
    per, bronze,
the reds and golds that drift around and through a
    salmon's

collective memory, fish transplanted from the other side
    of the land
to this distance of strange water. There's a bend

in the stream where they remember the rush
to the sweetness of milt over eggs although there's death in that
    push

to staying alive. Now you lean on his shoulder
like a child about to cry, trying to think how and where

and when to quietly
begin your journey.

Magical Thinking

You talk to yourself these days about yourself:
There is no baby here inside me.
Listen to me, walls, blue bed, white pages
of this chemistry book that tells no lies,

the sun flies down and lights on me alone.
I talk to myself these days about myself
because there's no one else
to listen to me. Walls, blue bed, white pages

on the desk beside the open window
where the sun flies down and lights on me alone,
soothe me in my sorrow, in my knowing
that there's no one else.

I have a lover. He says we're growing cells
near the desk beside the open window
where I sit reading *Paradiso, The Inferno*.
(Soothe me in my sorrow, in my knowing.)

It's not here, not in this world, I say,
although my lover says we're growing cells.
He says you're crazy, baby. Just get real.
I'm reading *Paradiso, The Inferno*.

If it's a hundred yesterdays ago today
it won't be there, not in this world, I say.
The first flower can wither in the frost.
He says you're crazy, baby. Just get real.

Listen to me, walls, blue bed, white pages.
These days I'm talking to myself about myself.

Into Ohio

Dry leaves blow across the road and scatter —
small animals running into the brittle grass —
and you lie down in the back seat of the car,
you lie and watch your lover's hooded face
in profile as he drives. You want to yell
at him again. He wants to hit you, hold you
down by both arms. This is not a fairy tale
where babies drift to shore in a canoe.

In the morning the doctor at the clinic
says it's way too late, he'd have to do a partial
birth abortion, drive through the brain a pick
and he won't. You see on the sonogram a girl
as she comes swirling up in the light of her bones,
waiting for the world's love, though she waits alone.

Christmas Night

God is in his house among the stars
so to God you cannot speak,
and your mother is cleaning up the leftovers.

Finding grace in the boughs of the dark
fir tree will not happen. You must go up step by step
to your bedroom, gather your blankets and a book.

Ponder the small life inside you with her occasional hiccup.
Whether to cross into the country of the blessed
and keep her — rattles, bells — or, lacking a map

of the dun plains, wander alone with the lost.
There is still time before the bud breaks from its caul
to save you both, to choose what is most

honest and simple. Downstairs the dishes rattle
in the dishwasher. Under your ribs the child's dance
is a samba. And now your mother comes and you can tell

her, you can help yourself to this glittering chance
wheeling just out of reach. When she asks you
Honey, are you pregnant? the irretrievable nonce

hangs in the air like a single flake of snow
you could catch on your tongue.
And you say No.

Sweater Villanelle

You think how good it is to be pregnant in winter,
since you're pregnant. You throw
a big woolly sweater, the one you call My Bear,

over your bulging belly as you drive the car
through a blizzard, the wild light-headedness of snow.
You think how good it is to be pregnant in winter

with all these flakes falling around you like the pure
covering of some religion. Are you cold with what you know
inside your woolly sweater? Can you bear

the knowing? A scarf hangs loosely from your shoulder
to conceal your engorged breasts. They hurt. The two
of you think how good it is to be pregnant in winter

so no one will guess: a down jacket or Gore-Tex outerwear
disguising the baby. You don't know yet how
in your big woolly sweater you will have to bear

down as your body lights up with a fire,
how the baby will drop so small and so blue
onto the cold tile in the hardness of winter,
how your big bloody sweater will hide what's bare.

Blowing Out the Candles

Snow falls like feathers outside the dorm window.
Breast feathers of towhees, feathers of snow

geese and trumpeter swans that fly for a winter's
warm weather cruise

over a pond in North Carolina.
White feathers and off-white feathers, a

fluttering before your eyes
taking you to a world without any purples, blues.

You wanted to keep the baby. He didn't.
He wanted to keep the baby. You didn't.

Your pink warm-ups hide you as you drink lemon
tea in the big chair beside the television.

When your mother drives over with a yellow-
frosted birthday cake, you pull the throw

closer to the hill of your secret.
Too long you pretended the pool inside was a late

period. You floated on that water as if the baby
might swim away.

He wanted to keep the baby. You didn't.
You wanted to keep the baby. He didn't.

There on your arm is yesterday's
beginning bruise.

You bumped the door, you tell your mother.
Then you blow out the candles of your future.

New World

Cut edges of diamonds   rain in the gutter
your body a ship   the last oak timber

creaking   your cargo shifts in the storm   get
under the covers   they're wet

he's scared says   he wants to go back to his dorm
not yet the baby is coming   *alarum*

as in Shakespeare   you were on Depo-Provera
Lady MacBeth   Desdemona

remember confusion rising through tears
when you danced with Madison   the car's

sleek gliding as you drove past the mall
her feet pushing inside you   it's a small dark baby girl

when you run to the bathroom
she drops into the oval bowl   your womb

is a seething ocean
all your oceans are pain

and you can't feel your feet
have they walked to another planet?

she's breathing there on the towels
when you clean her   blood on the tiles

little breaths like a wind that turns lightly
a prayer wheel   a leaf that's about to fly

green towels for wrapping her gurgle
then her silence   the bathtub full

of your grief   you hold the back of her head, her arm
he says he has to take a math exam

Born

So she comes with her little gasps and flutters.
Never a cry. The moment you wrap her in a towel
and lay her on the tiles of the bathroom floor

she sees the light of your hair

where a universe begins expanding.
Small finger clutches as if she were pulling up grass
while inside her eyelids float the thousands and thousands of seas.

Your mind is sheep's wool and fog.
When you carry her through the glass door
and throw her into the dark of the dumpster

she has already memorized every cell in both your bodies
like the stars in two skies.

Genetics

A mouse has done this, and the common swallow,
lemur catta. Among the leaves and grasses
they kill their young to keep tomorrow.
A mouse has done this and the common swallow.
You wrap your child in fear and instinct, sorrow,
place her deep where sunlight never passes.
A mouse has done this, and the common swallow,
lemur catta among the leaves and grasses.

Hormones

The taste of tin in your mouth vanishes
like snow on a crocus.

Your endocrine glands are opening up new trails —
estrogen, progesterone, bundles

of oxytocin, placental lactogen.
It's as if you've forgotten

the baby already, her search
for your nipple, her fingers' touch

on your breast, a thumb,
a mouth poised for colostrum.

Everything is flooding and receding, your tears a
torrent, and all the time the placenta

is still inside you. Blood in the toilet bowl,
blood on your thighs, and one red towel.

Where did you put her — Star, Little Tigress?
Why can't you remember where she is?

Mostly

Most of all, you want the bleeding to stop
and to wear your bikini in Florida,
delicate shells curled on the beach
inside each one a trickle of white sand,
sigh of palm trees over your head,
over your whole body the water in the pool spreading
nuances of blue and green and golden light.

Mostly you want to board Flight 387 with your father to
another world. You push the bikini's yellow stripes
down in the canvas bag, a tank top, shorts, as
if the clots weren't flowing deep
scarlet, your legs two riverbeds for streams
of what's still in you, what the baby lived in
growing all those months.

Mostly now, you want your lover to come back
and hold you, drive you, wrap you all in white.
Dream you didn't throw her to the dark. But
interns push your abdomen, a nurse waits
silently for what's to come. It feels like a fish
on a dock, sliding down the planks.
Nothing you tell the police makes any sense.

Strawberry Festival

It's hard to drag, this big
sack of what you should
have done.
— William Stafford

Your mother wears white linen,
brings you angel food and strawberries,
whipped cream over the top like every summer.

You're thinking how you could have placed her on a step.
You're wondering if a basket may have waited for your baby's
floating in a grassy river.

Or if some kind adopting couple might have written
the story of her life, a skein of sunny days
knitted to make her

years from now a sweet, unguessing woman.
You never dreamed of judges, courts, attorneys.
You never dreamed of murder.

He moves across the far sea of the lawn
to take your hand, gives it a gentle squeeze
to show he's still your Pastor.

Hiroshima was bombed long before you were born.
On the stone wall of the Sumitomo Bank somebody's
shape is etched by violent light.

You have become that figure.

Under Pisces

What do you pack when you leave for prison?
Outside your window snow piles higher on

the branches of the plum tree as in April
white petals will drift among the swell

of twigs like lovers with their tongues to the sun's
melting sky. You will not be anyone's.

Can you take your favorite bra?
Lace, satin, underwire adrift among bikini

panties? That shadow on the window is yours
and someone else's where light hovers

but will never throw its net again. Your swimming pool
is empty as your uterus is now, a bowl, a shell.

Will an orange jumpsuit compliment your skin,
the rasp of heavy nylon

against others in the prison van recall
the baby's last small gurgle?

It must be a little like skydiving.
You can take only one tangible thing

with you, a parachute. And hope.
Then the whole earth starts to hurtle up

into your face: a lake, two rivers, hills around Bedford,
stones becoming larger, leaves unblurred.

They'll inspect your duffelbag for drugs, look in
your mouth, the cave of your vagina for a weapon.

Can you take your eiderdown pillow,
sweet as the skin of sorrow,

soft as the ghost that goes with you everywhere?

The Inmate Remembers

The scent of roses
through my bedroom window made
me turn in sleep
to give more of my body.
It wasn't possible,
full as I was of
his wilderness already.
I wandered along a path
in bare feet,
their whorls and runes
marking where I went as if
it could be some totally different place.

꽃

In New York or Pennsylvania
someone is always hunting so
I had to keep my eyes
wide open (peeled, my grandmother
would say) when I was a kid
roaming the woods.
But from the corners where the lids meet
as in a kiss,
whenever I saw scarlet drop to snow
or fly to blue sky,
I never thought *cardinal*
but *that's what I want when I grow up*.
Flash and rapid, the sparkle everyone notices.
When the white wings of the amanita
unfurled from wet leaves where my feet
dug into the forest floor —
Death Angel —
I did not know those words.

Then I come to the Niagara River.
I lay my body down
in the current just above the falls
and let myself be swept
up to the edge,
go over the precipice,
plumage of peacocks, stars
in the water, collisions
of galaxies, atoms, animal eyes.
Who throws the white veil over me
making me a bride?
Who draws the white swirl of swords?
I come to the place where everything's
broken: bowls, timber, gutters,
kitchen sinks, a torn blue dress,
a piano and its threads of melody.
I can mend the song. I'll try.

Acknowledgments

I am profoundly grateful to those relatives who in their anguish related to me some of the story here. Also, to the reporters who covered the event for The Buffalo News, I owe another debt of gratitude. Beyond that, many if not most of the settings and particular details in these poems have been imagined.

To Sandra McPherson and Tess Gallagher, my loving thanks for the various wisdoms they brought to this manuscript.

Also, my thanks go to the editors of the following publications for including some of these poems:

Pontoon, The Floating Bridge Anthology: Hormones; Into Ohio
Margie: Blowing Out the Candles
Rose Alley Anthology: Magical Thinking